599
Ste

16668

STEELE, PHILIP
Killers: mammals

KILLERS

MAMMALS

PHILIP STEELE

Julian Messner

Copyright © 1991 by Julian Messner

First published by Heinemann Children's Reference,
a division of Heinemann Educational Books Ltd
Original Copyright © 1991 Heinemann Educational Books Ltd

JULIAN MESSNER and colophon are trademarks of
Simon & Schuster, Inc.
U.S. project editor: Nancy Furstinger

Printed in Hong Kong

Lib. ed. 10 9 8 7 6 5 4 3 2 1
Paper ed. 10 9 8 7 6 5 4 3 2 1

Library of Congress Cataloging-in-Publication Data
Steele, Philip.
  Killers: mammals/by Philip Steele.
    p. cm.
  Includes index
  Summary: Discusses mammals that can be harmful to humans and
  provides vital statistics on carnivores.
  1. Mammals – Juvenile literature. 2. Carnivora – Juvenile
  literature. 3. Dangerous animals –Juvenile literature.
  [1. Mammals. 2. Carnivores. 3. Dangerous animals.].
  I. Title.   90-19157
  QL706.2.S73 1991   CIP
  599.051–dc20   AC

  ISBN 0-671-72233-6 (LSB) ISBN 0-671-72234-4 (pbk).

Photographic acknowledgments
The author and publishers wish to acknowledge, with thanks, the following photographic sources:
a above *b* below *l* left *r* right
The cover photograph is courtesy of Frank Lane Photograph Agency (M Newman)
Camera Press pp22; 25*a*: Bruce Coleman pp13*a* (M. Price); 15 (I Erwin and Peggy Bauer); 21; 25*b* (Peter Jackson): Mary Evans Picture
Library p16: Eric and David Hosking pp10; 26; 27: Frank Lane Photograph Agency pp8 (M Newman); 6 (R S Virdee); 9*r* 11 (Peter Davey);
12 (Carlo Jeske); 14 (F Hartman); 19 23*a* (Merlyn Severn); 23*b* (Martin Withers); 28 (Peter Davey) 29*b* (C Dani & I Jeske): Mansell
Collection pp13*b*; 17*b*; 18; 20*b*; 29*a*: NHPA pp9*l*; 17*a* (P D Pickford); 20*a* (Manfred Doneggar); 30*l*; 31 (Martin Wendler); 30*r* (S Robinson)
The publishers have made every effort to trace the copyright holders, but if they have inadvertently overlooked any, they will be pleased
to make the necessary arrangement at the first opportunity.

CONTENTS

MEAT- OR PLANT-EATERS 6
Who's who 6
Why do mammals kill? 7
Attack and defense 7
DO NOT DISTURB 8
The world's biggest carnivore 8
Danger on the trail 9
An Arctic hunter 9
A POWERFUL HUNTER 10
Ambush on the plains 10
A threat to humans 11
SUPERCATS! 12
Stalkers of the jungle 12
The hunter hunted 13
People as prey 13
TREETOP KILLERS 14
The South American spitfire 15
The fastest hunter 15
HOWLING AT THE MOON 16
Mad dog disease 16
The big, bad wolf 17
Hunting with the pack 17

DEATH BY PLAGUE 18
The vampires 19
WHEN PIGS RUN WILD 20
A forest life 20
STAMPEDE! 22
Death in the arena 23
Old bulls 23
CHARGE OF THE HEAVIES 24
A rhino's weapons 24
Fast and unpredictable 25
At risk 25
ROLLING IN MUD 26
Armor and tusks 27
Hippo attack 27
KILLERS — OR GENTLE GIANTS? 28
The largest land mammals 28
Giant apes 29
The ocean giants 29
SAVING THE MAMMALS 30
Sport? 31
A changing landscape 31
A new world 31
Index 32

MEAT- OR PLANT- EATERS

THE world of nature is often violent. Many animals must kill in order to live. These animals are meat-eaters, or carnivores. Other animals are plant-eaters, or herbivores. Many of these are killed and eaten by carnivores.

The feeding habits of animals are linked together, forming "food chains." Each form of life depends on another for its survival. Most animals kill only what they can eat. If they killed too much, the animals they hunted, called prey, might disappear.

Lioness with prey

★ **A mammal is any animal that gives birth to live young. Its young feed on milk.**

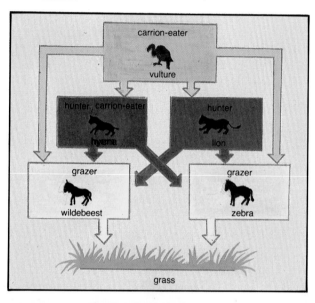

WHO'S WHO

THIS book is about mammals. There are 4,230 different kinds, or species, of mammals. Only a few of these are dangerous to humans. The mammal species is divided into 19 large groups, or orders. For example, humans and apes belong to the order known as primates.

WHY DO MAMMALS KILL?

A FEW mammals sometimes kill humans and eat them. Other animals are only dangerous when they are defending themselves or their young. Still other animals are dangerous to humans indirectly. For example, rats can pass on deadly diseases if they bite someone.

ATTACK AND DEFENSE

O VER the ages, each species of mammal has developed weapons they can use in attack and defense. Many have sharp claws for scratching, or strong hooves for kicking. Some have pointed horns or tusks for stabbing, or daggerlike teeth for biting.

Sometimes mammals have thick armor-plating or sharp spines or quills.

Horses have strong hooves.

Highland cattle have pointed horns.

Leopards have long front teeth.

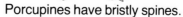
Porcupines have bristly spines.

DO NOT DISTURB

E VERYBODY likes cuddly toy bears. Real bears, however, can be very dangerous. They are slow-moving, flat-footed animals that can rear up on their hind legs. They have sharp teeth, long claws, and great strength. Bears are classed as carnivores. Actually, most species will eat anything, including insects, fish, roots, honeycombs, and berries.

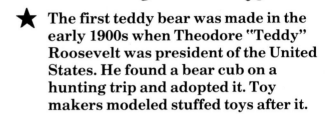

★ The first teddy bear was made in the early 1900s when Theodore "Teddy" Roosevelt was president of the United States. He found a bear cub on a hunting trip and adopted it. Toy makers modeled stuffed toys after it.

THE WORLD'S BIGGEST CARNIVORE

T HE brown bear is found in North America and in parts of Europe and Asia. The grizzly and the Kodiak bear belong to this species. The Kodiak bear is named for the island near Alaska where most of them live. It can weigh 1,650 pounds and measure more than 13 feet from nose to tail. Most males weigh about 1,100 pounds and measure about 8 feet long. The Kodiak bear is the largest meat-eating creature on land.

Kodiak bears

8

DANGER ON THE TRAIL

I F you have ever been to Yellowstone National Park in Wyoming, you have seen signs warning you about bears. The bears come to campsites and search for food. If they are left alone they will wander away. If they are scared or cornered they may attack. One swipe of a bear's paw can kill a human.

caution
RECENT BEAR SIGHTINGS IN AREA

AN ARCTIC HUNTER

O NE of the most beautiful bears of all is also one of the most feared. The polar bear of the Arctic Circle has cream-colored fur that blends in with the ice and snow. These animals are nimble and very strong. Most males weigh about 880 pounds.

Polar bears are tireless hunters. They track prey over great distances, swimming with ease and resting on ice floes. Their front paws are webbed and are designed to grip slippery ice. Polar bears usually eat seals, but they may also kill people. Males are particularly dangerous during the mating season.

Polar bears

A POWERFUL HUNTER

A LION cub may act as playful as a kitten. However, the cub's games are teaching it how to hunt and kill when it grows up.

An adult lion weighs about 550 pounds. It may be 3¼ feet high and 9 feet long. Its body is muscular and very strong. One blow from a lion's paw can break the neck of an antelope or a zebra. Its claws can rip through flesh, and its teeth and strong jaws can crack bones.

AMBUSH ON THE PLAINS

A LION has a tan-colored coat. This makes it hard to see against the dusty African plains where it lives. Female lions do most of the hunting. Several hunt together. Some of them circle behind a herd and drive the animals toward the rest of the lions. A victim is singled out and killed. Then the whole family, or pride, gathers and feeds on the prey until they can eat no more.

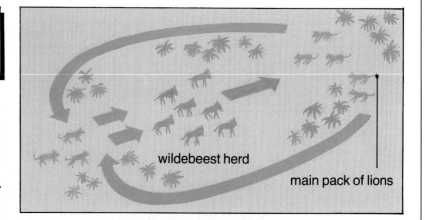

wildebeest herd

main pack of lions

A pride of lions

A THREAT TO HUMANS

L IONS do not usually attack people. Scientists studying lions have lived with them and befriended them. However, all lions are dangerous when they are cornered or wounded. Often old, bad-tempered male lions living alone will kill humans. One killed 40 people. Usually these lions are hunted and killed.

King of the beasts

The lion is often called the "king of beasts." It is chosen as a symbol for countries and royal families. However, the lion has been hunted and killed by humans for hundreds of years. Today a few lions live in Asia and most live in Africa. Once large numbers of lions lived in Europe and Asia, and many more in Africa.

SUPERCATS!

MOST tigers are about 10 feet long. Like lions, they have sharp claws, powerful limbs, and fierce jaws. Tigers slink more than lions. All tigers are found in Asia.

STALKERS OF THE JUNGLE

TIGERS have gold-colored coats with dark stripes. Many live in forests or on the grasslands. Their stripes help them to hide in the shadows and undergrowth. Tigers rest during the day and hunt at dusk.

★ **An adult tiger can eat up to 55 pounds of meat at once.**

THE HUNTER HUNTED

H UMANS have hunted the tiger and cut down the forests where it lives. About a hundred years ago it was popular for Europeans to shoot tigers in India. As a result, thousands were killed, and tigers have become very rare. India, Nepal, and Bangladesh have set aside land where tigers can live in safety. Tigers are also being studied to learn more about them.

Attaching a radio-collar to a tigress in Nepal

PEOPLE AS PREY

H UMANS are easy prey for tigers that are old or injured. Some tigers are said to have killed hundreds of people before they were killed. These figures are hard to know for sure because attacks often happen in remote areas. Many attacks still occur in the Sundarbans swamps between India and Bangladesh.

TREETOP KILLERS

LEOPARDS live in Africa and southern Asia. They have tan-colored fur with black, rose-shaped markings. Some are completely black. They are known as panthers. Male leopards can grow up to 8 feet long, and weigh about 100 pounds.

Leopards hunt on their own. They kill baboons, deer, and antelope, and will attack farm dogs and livestock. They crush the prey's skull or rip open the throat. Then they drag the body into the fork of a tree and eat it leisurely.

Leopards have one of the worst records of attacking people. Some are known to have killed up to 400 humans apiece. Humans have an even worse record of killing leopards. They have shot these beautiful cats by the thousands.

THE SOUTH AMERICAN SPITFIRE

THE jaguar looks like the leopard. It, too, has tan-colored fur with rose-shaped markings. However, a central black spot is missing from the leopard's markings. Most jaguars live in Central and South America. A few live in the southern United States.

The jaguar is built more solidly than the leopard. It is the biggest cat in the Americas. Males weigh between 120 and 240 pounds, and are up to 9 feet long. The jaguar is a powerful animal with sharp teeth and claws.

Jaguars hunt alone, covering an area of about 4 square miles. They mostly live in forests and can swim and climb trees in search of prey. Their spotted coat helps to hide them among the leaves and spotted patterns of the forest floor.

Jaguars eat monkeys, the giant rodents called capybaras, the pig-like peccaries, and cattle. They are fierce hunters and will even tackle alligators. They also catch fish with their paws.

Killer or victim?
The jaguar has a reputation for killing people, but it is not a fair one. In the past the jaguar has been hunted for its fur. Also, when it is wounded or provoked, it will attack people and kill them. There are stories of jaguars regularly killing people. However, there are actually very few records of this.

THE FASTEST HUNTER

THE cheetah lives in Africa and Asia, where it is very rare. It is a large cat, more than 6½ feet from nose to tip of tail. Its body is slim and is built for speed. It can run at up to 70 miles an hour for a short time.

HOWLING AT THE MOON

W HEN the first hunters made their camps, wolves and jackals would come looking for scraps of meat. Humans soon found that they could tame the pups and train them to hunt.

The first tame dogs were bred about 12,000 years ago. Over the ages dogs were trained to herd animals, bring back game, guard buildings, and fight in battles. Other dogs were bred only for their good looks and did no work at all.

MAD DOG DISEASE

D OGS can be dangerous to humans, but not because they are fierce by nature. It is because they can carry a disease called rabies. Foxes often contract rabies and pass it on to pet dogs. The sick animal is paralyzed. It twitches, foams at the mouth, and cannot eat or drink. Humans who are bitten by a dog with rabies may die if they are not treated in time.

To prevent the spread of rabies, dogs are annually vaccinated against the disease. Dogs taken to another country are kept apart until officials are sure they do not carry rabies.

★ **The dingo is an Australian dog with a light brown coat. It is probably descended from tame dogs brought to Australia about 3,000 years ago. Today it runs wild. It hunts kangaroos and wallabies, and raids sheep farms. It hunts in small groups. Dingoes are usually not dangerous to humans.**

THE BIG, BAD WOLF

I N fairy tales the wolf is often a savage creature with big fangs and a long, red tongue. People have feared these wild members of the dog family for hundreds of years.

In reality, wolves are shy. They are expert hunters, but they only attack humans if they are cornered or scared. Usually, wolves run away when they meet people.

One kind of wolf, the gray wolf, is about 6 feet long, including its tail, and weighs about 110 pounds. It hunts alone or in packs, and can track its prey over great distances. It kills deer, hares, and livestock.

HUNTING WITH THE PACK

M ANY members of the dog family are fierce hunters. The Cape hunting dog of Africa is about 4 feet from nose to tail and weighs up to 100 pounds. It has a spotted coat, a long bushy tail, and big ears. It also has powerful jaws and strong teeth for cracking bones. It hunts in packs. It usually eats antelope or zebra. Hunting dogs rarely attack humans.

DEATH BY PLAGUE

T HE mouse family has many members. Most of them are small, furry, and cute. The brown rat and the black rat, however, are aggressive and dangerous to humans. They may bite people with their large front teeth and cause infection. They get into stored food and pollute it with their droppings. If people eat this spoiled food, they may get food poisoning. They may even die.

Rats carry disease. The tiny oriental rat flea sometimes is found in the fur of rats. It passes on a disease called bubonic plague. The flea bites a rat infected with the disease. Then it passes on the disease when it bites a human. With modern medicine and pest control, bubonic plague is now rare.

The Black Death

In 1348 the worst outbreak of plague occurred in Europe. It was called the Black Death. About 25 million people died. In London's Great Plague of 1665, thousands died and were buried in mass graves. Between 1896 and 1917, the plague killed more than 10 million people in India.

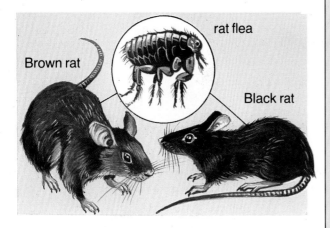

★ **Rats carry several killer diseases.**

Plague victims being buried, London, 1665

THE VAMPIRES

O horror film is complete without flocks of bats flying down from gloomy-looking ruins. In reality, bats are seldom harmful. However, the common vampire bats of Central and South America can be dangerous. Their upper teeth are long and sharp. They bite their victim and drink large amounts of its blood. Sometimes they drink until they are bloated. A chemical in the bats' saliva stops the blood from clotting.

Vampire bats usually attack animals such as cattle and horses. However, sometimes they attack people while they sleep. They make a wound in their toes and drink their blood. The danger from vampire bats does not come from the loss of blood. Rather, it comes from the diseases they carry, particularly rabies. Vampire bats kill thousands of cattle each year. Occasionally a human dies as well.

WHEN PIGS RUN WILD

W E think of farm animals as being completely tame. However, their wild ancestors were often very aggressive.

The first pigs in Europe were descended from the wild boars of Europe and Asia. Later, these pigs were bred with heavier Chinese breeds.

The wild boar is a hairy pig. Its upper front teeth curve upward and outward. They form sharp tusks up to 1 foot long.

★ **The wild boar is about 6 feet long and can weigh up to 496 pounds.**

A FOREST LIFE

B OARS live in forests, where they dig up plants and acorns for food. They are usually harmless, but they can be dangerous when they are disturbed or scared. Then they may charge. They may cut people with their tusks and may break limbs.

People sometimes died while hunting boars in the Middle Ages. They used long spears with crossbars to stop a charging boar.

A boar hunt

STAMPEDE!

CATTLE may be the most dangerous animal we have tamed. Cows are gentle, but bulls are often bad-tempered and very strong. The heaviest farm breed can weigh almost 4,000 pounds and one African breed has horns more than 9 feet long!

An angry bull may charge at people and toss them with its horns. Large numbers of cattle being moved together may get scared. They may stampede, or charge blindly, and trample people.

Buffalo herd

DEATH IN THE ARENA

I N some countries, bullfights are popular. A bull is released into an arena. Men wave capes at the bull to make it angry. Then a matador tries to kill it. Sometimes he is tossed by the bull's horns and gored to death.

OLD BULLS

A FRICANS probably fear the Cape buffalo more than any other animal. Herds may run away when disturbed, but old bulls often fight. When they charge, they cannot be stopped. They may weigh a ton, and their curved horns can be 4½ feet long. Bulls will chase people and trample them to death.

CHARGE OF THE HEAVIES

HINOCEROSES usually are not dangerous. They cannot see very well, and they move slowly over the land, eating plants. However, when they are disturbed they can turn mean and chase the intruder.

★ **The name rhinoceros means "horned nose."**

A RHINO'S WEAPONS

HINOS have one or two horns on their snout. These spikes are not made of bone. They are made of tough, matted fiber. The Asian rhinos also have long lower teeth that can be deadly. All rhinos have a thick, tough hide. The hide of the great Indian rhino is bumpy and has deep folds.

White rhino

Indian rhino

Black rhino

How much does a rhino weigh?
The Sumatran rhino weighs about ½ ton, the Javan 1 ton, and the great Indian 2½ tons. The Black rhino weighs 1½ tons and the White rhino 3 tons.

24

FAST AND UNPREDICTABLE

IF rhinos are attacked, they may get nervous. It is hard to know how they will react. Rhinos may have poor eyesight, but their other senses are sharp. When they are angry, they will charge at speeds of up to 31 miles an hour. They can turn around quickly. The Black rhino will even charge at a jeep, and can overturn it.

A charging Black rhino

The Kenyan anti-poaching squad discovers a dead rhino

AT RISK

ALL five rhino species are in danger of dying out. They have been hunted for years. Although rhinos are protected in game parks, hunters sneak in and kill them.

ROLLING IN MUD

THE word hippopotamus means "river horse," but these huge creatures are more like pigs. Two species live in Africa. The pygmy hippopotamus weighs up to 500 pounds and is about 6 feet long. The common hippopotamus is about 3,500 pounds but can weigh more than 2½ tons. It is about 11½ feet long.

Large groups of hippos live in the swamps of southern Sudan. During the day they stay in the water. After the sun sets, they go ashore to eat and roll on the muddy banks. They mostly eat plants.

Hippos face an uncertain future. The rivers and swamps where they live are often drained or dammed for irrigation.

ARMOR AND TUSKS

H IPPOPOTAMUS hide is thick, and protects the body during fights. Their teeth are fierce looking. The lower front teeth are the largest. They form tusks that may grow to be between 2 and 5 feet long and weigh more than 2 pounds each. The tusks never stop growing. They grind against the upper teeth and become sharp.

HIPPOPOTAMUS ATTACK

H IPPOPOTAMUSES are slow-moving animals and are rarely aggressive. However, males fight each other during the mating season. They use their tusks to cut the rival hippo's flesh.

Old males that have been driven out of a group are often bad-tempered. An angry old hippo may attack a canoe, overturning and smashing it.

Hippos may also become aggressive when defending their young, or if they are disturbed when eating. Hippos are surprisingly fast on land. They can easily catch up with somebody running away.

27

KILLERS-OR GENTLE GIANTS?

S OME mammals are so big that few animals threaten them. Also, they eat plants, so they do not kill prey. However, because they are big, they may be dangerous anyway.

THE LARGEST LAND MAMMALS

T HERE are two species of elephant. A male or "bull" African elephant can grow to 13 feet high and weigh 10 tons. Most are only half this weight though. The Indian elephant is not as big as the African and has smaller ears.

Elephants are gentle, intelligent animals that eat plants. They are often friendly toward humans. In fact the Indian elephant has been tamed and trained to haul logs. However, humans have rarely treated elephants well. Although they are protected by law, the African elephants are brutally hunted for their long tusks. These are used to make ivory ornaments.

The tusks are really huge upper teeth. They grow into long, curving spikes up to 8 feet in length. Elephants use them for digging and for pushing over trees. If an elephant becomes angry, the tusks become deadly weapons.

Old bull elephants are often bad-tempered. When attacked or frightened though, any elephant may become violent. They raise their huge, flapping ears, lift their trunks, and roar loudly. Then they charge.

A young African elephant

GIANT APES

G ORILLAS are the biggest apes in the world. They live in the forests of Africa. A male weighs about 450 pounds and is 5½ feet tall.

Gorillas are peaceful, intelligent plant-eaters. Although they are very strong and may charge at an intruder, they will probably only bite.

THE OCEAN GIANTS

T HE biggest mammals of all live in the sea. Whales are not fishes, although they look like them. They breathe air and feed their young with milk. The largest is the Blue whale, which can be about 85 feet long and weigh more than 100 tons. This huge mammal eats only tiny shrimps.

Whales are harmless and are among the most intelligent creatures on Earth. However, they have been hunted for oil, blubber, and meat until many species are nearly extinct. In the nineteenth century, sailors hunted whales from long rowing boats, using harpoons. Many people drowned, because whales often smashed the boats or pulled the boats under as they dove.

Today, laws control the amount of whaling that is carried out in the world. However, many whales are still killed. They are tracked with electronic equipment. Then they are killed from a distance with explosive harpoons.

SAVING THE MAMMALS

MANY mammals are able to kill people. Most of them only do so when they are attacked and threatened. However, one species of mammal not only kills other creatures for pleasure, it is able to kill every living thing on the planet. It is the human being.

Human beings hunt other mammals for food. They hunt them for other reasons as well. Elephants are killed so that ivory chess pieces can be made from their tusks. Jaguars are shot so that their skins can be made into fur coats. Rhinos are killed because people wrongly believe that the ground-up horn can help heal when it is added to medicines.

Elephant tusks and rhino horns

Poachers with a jaguar

Animals that compete with humans for food are killed. Sea otters and seals are slaughtered because people claim that these mammals steal fish.

SPORT?

HUMANS are often cruel in the name of sport. They tease bulls to make them angry and then kill them in front of a large crowd. They force dogs or gamecocks to fight, and they bet on the results. They also capture wild animals for zoos and pet shops, and ship them in airless crates where many die from lack of air.

A caged puma

A CHANGING LANDSCAPE

MANY mammals are threatened with extinction because humans have cleared forests, drained swamps, or poisoned rivers and seas with chemicals. Because their natural environment has been destroyed or been reduced, these mammals cannot survive.

★ Fifty years ago, there were 20 times more tigers in India than there are today.

★ The number of Blue whales has declined from about 200,000 to 5,000.

★ There are fewer than 200 Sumatran rhinoceroses left alive in the world today.

A NEW WORLD

HUMANS' intelligence enabled us to become better at killing than any other creature. Fortunately, our intelligence is now being used to save mammals from extinction.

All over the world people are working hard to save endangered species. Laws are being passed making it illegal to kill them.

Even if a mammal is a killer, we must protect it and its habitat. Each species depends on others for its survival. We must learn to share our planet with other species so that we ourselves will survive.

31

INDEX

Africa 10, 11, 14, 15, 16, 22, 23, 26, 29, 31
African elephant 28
Alaska 8
Amazonian rain forest 19
America
  Central 15, 19
  North 8, 9
  South 15, 19
apes 6, 29
Asia 8, 11, 12, 14, 15, 20, 24
Asian rhino 24
Australia 16

Bangladesh 13
bats 19
bears 8, 9
Black Death 18
black rat 18
Black rhino 24
blood 15, 19
Blue whale 29, 31
brown bear 8
brown rat 18
bubonic plague 18
bullfights 23
bulls 22, 23, 31

Cape buffalo 7, 23
Cape hunting dog 17
cattle 22
cheetahs 15
claws 7, 8, 9, 10, 12, 15
common hippo 26
common vampire bat 19

dingoes 16
disease 7, 16, 18
dogs 16, 31

elephants 28, 30, 31
Europe 8, 11, 18, 20

food networks 6
fur 15, 30

game parks 25
gorillas 29
Great Plague 18
gray wolf 17
grizzly bear 8

hippopotamuses 26, 27
hooves 7
horns 7, 22, 23, 24
humans 6, 7, 13, 14, 15, 16, 17, 18, 19, 23,
  30, 31
hunting 9, 10, 12, 14, 15, 17, 20, 25, 29

India 13, 18, 31
Indian elephant 28
Indian rhino 24

jaguars 15, 30
Jarvan rhino 24

Kodiak bear 8
Kodiak Island 8

leopards 14
lions 6, 7, 10, 31

man-eaters 11, 14, 15
Middle Ages 16, 20

Nepal 13

panthers 14
pigs 20
poachers 31
Polar bear 9
pgymy hippo 26

rabies 16, 19
rat flea 18
rats 6, 7, 18
rhinoceroses 24, 25, 30
rodents 6
Roosevelt, President 8
Russia 17

Siberian tiger 12
stampede 22
Sudan 26
Sumatran rhino 24, 31
Surdarbans swamps 13

teeth 7, 8, 10, 15, 17, 18,-19, 20, 24, 27, 28
tigers 6, 7, 12, 13, 31
tusks 7, 20, 27, 28

United States 15

vampire bat 19

whales 29, 31
whaling 29
White rhino 24
wild boars 20
wolves 16, 17
Wyoming 9

Yellowstone National Park 9